BEST
DUMP
CAKES
EVER

BEST DUMP CAKES EVER

BEST
DUMP
CAKES
EVER

MIND-BLOWINGLY EASY
DUMP-AND-BAKE
CAKE-MIX DESSERTS

monica sweeney

Dump Cakes photo credits

All photography by Allan Penn unless otherwise indicated, below:

Best Dump Cakes Ever
ISBN: 978-1-58157270-4

Published by The Countryman Press, P.O. Box 748, Woodstock, VT 05091

Distributed by W. W. Norton & Company, Inc., 500 Fifth Avenue, New York, NY 10110

Printed in the United States

10 9 8 7 6 5 4

TO HOLLY SCHMIDT AND ALLAN PENN.
WITH ALL OF YOUR SUPPORT,
THIS BOOK FELT LIKE IT WROTE ITSELF.

BEST DUMP CAKES EVER
CONTENTS

Chapter Two: Chocolatey Cakes / 74

Chapter Three: Sauces and Toppings / 102

What Is a Dump Cake?

Dump cakes may not have the most appealing name, but they are amazingly delicious and a huge time-saver for bakers! Rather than measure, mix, and bake cakes from scratch, using all kinds of bowls and spoons and measuring cups, you simply spread some basic ingredients in a 9 × 13-inch pan and throw it in the oven, where a miracle occurs. After 30 or 40 minutes, you have an impressive dessert that tastes like it took hours to make! Dump cakes are a creative way to dress up plain old cake mix into something really special, and are easy enough for a child to make.

In this book, I'll show you how to make both fruit dump cakes and chocolate dump cakes. The fruit cakes start with canned pie filling, or in some cases canned fruit, which you spread on the bottom of a greased 9 × 13-inch pan. Then you sprinkle a box of cake mix on top of the fruit, and the whole thing is topped with slices of butter. In the oven, the butter melts on the top and the fruit bubbles up from the bottom, causing the cake mix to transform into a cobbler-like topping. A couple of the recipes call for using soda instead of the butter on the top, which creates a sweeter flavor and slightly different texture. You can play around with both and see which you like better, and any of the recipes can be adapted to your preference. If you prefer using soda, just substitute 12 ounces of your favorite soda for the butter in the recipe.

Most of the chocolate dump cakes involve a different process, but one that is just as easy. They start with chocolate instant pudding mix, which you stir together with milk. Then you stir the chocolate cake mix into the pudding to create a thick chocolate cake batter. This is spread in the pan, topped with nuts, chocolate chips, or other toppings, and baked until set. The chocolate dump cakes have a fudgy, rich texture that is like a cross between a brownie and cake.

As you head off into your dump cake adventure, don't be afraid to be creative! If you like blueberries better than cherries, feel free to make the swap! All of these recipes are very forgiving and easy to suit to your family's tastes. So experiment away, and enjoy!

BEST
DUMP
CAKES
EVER

CHAPTER ONE

FRUITY CAKES

Pineapple Macadamia Nut

A Hawaiian island in a dessert! The sunny flavor of pineapple and the decadent crunch of macadamia nuts will make you feel the warm ocean breeze, even in the dead of winter.

2 (16-ounce) cans crushed pineapple

1 box yellow cake mix

1/2 cup chopped macadamia nuts

1/2 cup butter, sliced into 12 thin slices

Preheat the oven to 350 degrees F. Grease a 9 × 13-inch pan. Spread the pineapple on the bottom of the pan. Sprinkle the cake mix over the pineapple. Top with the macadamia nuts. Evenly place the butter slices on top and bake for 45 minutes or until the cake is golden brown and the fruit is bubbling.

"Cooking is like love. It should be entered into with abandon or not at all."
—Harriet Van Horne

Pineapple Banana

Pineapple and banana are a great combination (both grow in the tropics, after all!), and this cake couldn't be easier to put together. You can add coconut or chopped nuts to the top if you want to make it extra fancy, but the sweet, simple flavor is wonderful just as it is.

2 (16-ounce) cans crushed pineapple

1 box banana cake mix

1/2 cup butter, sliced into 12 thin slices

Preheat the oven to 350 degrees F. Grease a 9 × 13-inch pan. Spread the pie filling on the bottom of the pan. Sprinkle the cake mix over the fruit. Evenly place the butter slices on top. Bake for 35 to 40 minutes or until the cake is golden and the fruit is bubbling.

Piña Colada

A simple and satisfying tropical treat! The shredded coconut will toast in the oven, releasing flavor and becoming lightly browned. If you are a real coconut lover, make this with coconut cake mix. If you prefer the taste of vanilla, use yellow or white cake mix. It is up to you!

2 (16-ounce) cans crushed pineapple

1 box coconut, yellow, or white cake mix

1/2 cup butter, sliced into 12 thin slices

1 cup shredded sweetened coconut

Preheat the oven to 350 degrees F. Grease a 9 × 13-inch pan. Spread the pineapple on the bottom of the pan. Sprinkle the cake mix over the pineapple. Evenly place the butter slices on top and finish with shredded coconut. Bake for 35 to 40 minutes or until the cake and coconut are golden brown and the fruit is bubbling.

Cherry Berry

A bright and cheerful treat with the added bonus of lots of antioxidants from the berries! This cake combines pie filling with frozen berries for a fresh-tasting treat you can enjoy all year round.

1 (21-ounce) can cherry pie filling

1 (15-ounce) bag frozen mixed berries

1 box white cake mix

1/2 cup butter, sliced into 12 thin slices

Preheat the oven to 350 degrees F. Grease a 9 × 13-inch pan. Spread the cherry pie filling on the bottom of the pan. Top with the mixed berries. Sprinkle the cake mix over the fruit. Evenly place the butter slices on top. Bake for 45 to 55 minutes or until the cake is golden and the fruit is bubbling.

"A boy doesn't have to go to war to be a hero; he can say he doesn't like pie when he sees there isn't enough to go around."

—E. W. Howe

Blueberry Vanilla

A simple take on classic blueberry pie, this three-ingredient dump cake allows you to throw together an impressive dessert in no time! For a fresher berry flavor, add a bag of frozen wild blueberries before you sprinkle the cake mix.

2 (21-ounce) cans blueberry pie filling

1 (12-ounce) bag frozen wild blueberries (optional)

1 box vanilla cake mix

1/2 cup butter, sliced into 12 thin slices

Preheat the oven to 350 degrees F. Grease a 9 × 13-inch pan. Spread the pie filling on the bottom of the pan. Add the frozen blueberries, if using. Sprinkle the cake mix over the fruit. Evenly place the butter slices on top. Bake for 35 to 40 minutes (45 to 55 minutes if you used frozen berries) or until the cake is golden and the fruit is bubbling.

"Cut my pie into four pieces, I don't think I could eat eight."   —Yogi Berra

Peach Melba

Frozen raspberries lend a fresh-from-the-garden flavor to this elegant dessert. This is sublime topped with vanilla ice cream, and nobody will judge you if you eat it for breakfast. It is fruit, after all!

2 (15-ounce) cans sliced or chunked peaches in heavy syrup

1 (12-ounce) bag frozen raspberries

1 box vanilla cake mix

1/2 cup butter, sliced into 12 thin slices

Preheat the oven to 350 degrees F. Grease a 9 × 13-inch pan. Spread the peaches on the bottom of the pan. Top with the raspberries. Sprinkle the cake mix over the fruit. Evenly place the butter slices on top. Bake for 45 to 55 minutes or until the cake is golden and the fruit is bubbling.

Apple Cinnamon

This delicious treat puts other apple cobblers to shame, and it could not be easier! It is great for crisp fall days, and elegant enough to serve with Thanksgiving dinner.

2 (21-ounce) cans apple pie filling

1 box vanilla cake mix

1 tablespoon granulated sugar

1/2 teaspoon cinnamon

1/2 cup butter, sliced into 12 thin slices

Preheat the oven to 350 degrees F. Grease a 9 × 13-inch pan. Spread the apple pie filling on the bottom of the pan. Sprinkle the cake mix over the fruit. Sprinkle the sugar and cinnamon on top of the cake mix. Evenly place the butter slices on top. Bake for 35 to 40 minutes or until the cake is golden and the fruit is bubbling.

"Good apple pies are a considerable part of our domestic happiness."
—Jane Austen

Pear Ginger

A simple three-ingredient cake that nevertheless tastes like it took all day! The warm, spicy gingerbread is the ideal complement to the sweet pears, and will make this a favorite for all the gingersnap lovers in your house.

2 (15-ounce) cans sliced pears in heavy syrup

1 box gingerbread cake mix

1/2 cup butter, sliced into 12 thin slices

Preheat the oven to 350 degrees F. Grease a 9 × 13-inch pan. Spread the canned pears on the bottom of the pan. Sprinkle the cake mix over the fruit. Evenly place the butter slices on top. Bake for 35 to 40 minutes or until the cake is golden and the fruit is bubbling.

Pumpkin Spice

I absolutely love anything pumpkin—pumpkin lattes, pumpkin cookies, and most of all, this super-simple Pumpkin Spice Dump Cake! While this is perfect for fall (it's great for a Halloween party), you can buy pumpkin pie filling year-round, so you can enjoy it anytime.

2 (15-ounce) cans pumpkin pie filling

1 box vanilla cake mix

1/2 cup butter, sliced into 12 thin slices

1 teaspoon pumpkin pie spice

1 tablespoon granulated sugar

Preheat the oven to 350 degrees F. Grease a 9 × 13-inch pan. Spread the pumpkin pie filling on the bottom of the pan. Sprinkle the cake mix over the pumpkin. Evenly place the butter slices on top. Mix the pumpkin pie spice and sugar together and sprinkle on top. Bake for 35 to 40 minutes or until the cake is golden and the fruit is bubbling.

"Life starts all over again when it gets crisp in the fall."   —F. Scott Fitzgerald

Apple Caramel Pecan

This decadent cake is a sweet, sticky caramel fantasy come true! The crunch of pecans adds textural contrast, and the drizzle of caramel sauce on top heightens the delicious butterscotch flavor. If you can't find caramel cake mix, substitute vanilla.

2 (21-ounce) cans apple pie filling

1 box caramel cake mix

1/2 cup butter, sliced into 12 thin slices

1/2 cup chopped pecans

1/2 cup caramel sauce

Preheat the oven to 350 degrees F. Grease a 9 × 13-inch pan. Spread the pie filling on the bottom of the pan. Sprinkle the cake mix over the pie filling. Place the butter slices evenly on top and sprinkle the pecans over the butter. Drizzle the caramel sauce on top. Bake for 35 to 40 minutes or until the cake is golden and the fruit is bubbling.

"One of the very nicest things about life is the way we must regularly stop whatever it is we are doing and devote our attention to eating."

—Luciano Pavarotti

Strawberry

A strawberry lover's dream! This wonderful cake has three different layers of strawberry flavor—the pie filling, the cake mix, and the frozen strawberries all offer a different hit of the bright red fruit's sunny sweetness, and the red and pink colors make it especially festive.

2 (21-ounce) cans strawberry pie filling

1 box strawberry cake mix

1 (14-ounce) bag frozen sliced strawberries

1/4 cup granulated sugar

1/2 cup butter, sliced into 12 thin slices

Preheat the oven to 350 degrees F. Grease a 9 × 13-inch pan. Spread the pie filling on the bottom of the pan. Sprinkle the cake mix over the pie filling. Spread the frozen strawberries on top and evenly sprinkle the sugar over the strawberries. Place the butter slices evenly on top. Bake for 35 to 40 minutes or until the cake is golden and the fruit is bubbling.

Lemon Blueberry Corn Bread

This home-style cake features the crunch of cornmeal along with the bright flavor of lemon to perfectly complement juicy blueberries. It would be just as much at home on the breakfast table as the dessert table, and makes a stunning brunch treat. Try making it with blackberry pie filling if you can find it!

2 (21-ounce) cans blueberry pie filling

1 (8.5-ounce) box corn bread or corn muffin mix

1/2 box lemon cake mix

1/2 cup butter, sliced into 12 thin slices

Preheat the oven to 350 degrees F. Grease a 9 × 13-inch pan. Spread the pie filling on the bottom of the pan. Sprinkle the corn bread and cake mixes evenly over the fruit. Place the butter slices evenly on top. Bake for 35 to 40 minutes or until the cake is golden and the fruit is bubbling.

Pumpkin Gingerbread

Another great flavor combination—pumpkin and gingerbread! This cake tastes like autumn on a plate, and is perfect for fans of pumpkin spice everything. The gingerbread adds a spicy note that pairs perfectly with the pumpkin flavor. This one requires a little mixing before you add it to the pan, but it is worth the extra step!

1 (15-ounce) can pumpkin puree

1 (10-ounce) can evaporated milk

1 cup light brown sugar

3 large eggs

2 teaspoons pumpkin pie spice

1 box gingerbread cake mix

1 cup butter, melted

Preheat the oven to 350 degrees F. Grease a 9 × 13-inch pan. Mix the pumpkin puree, evaporated milk, brown sugar, eggs, and pumpkin pie spice together in a bowl. Spread this mixture in the prepared pan. Sprinkle the cake mix evenly on top, and then drizzle the melted butter over everything. Bake for 35 to 40 minutes or until the cake is golden and the fruit is bubbling.

"I'm so glad I live in a world where there are Octobers."
—L. M. Montgomery, *Anne of Green Gables*

Strawberry Banana

If strawberry banana is your favorite yogurt or smoothie flavor, you will love this cake! It couldn't be simpler, and the banana cake really helps the sweet strawberries shine. If you want to amp up the banana flavor, slice a fresh banana on top of the strawberries before you add the cake mix.

2 (21-ounce) cans strawberry pie filling

1 box banana cake mix

1/2 cup butter, sliced into 12 thin slices

Preheat the oven to 350 degrees F. Grease a 9 × 13-inch pan. Spread the pie filling on the bottom of the pan. Sprinkle the cake mix evenly over the fruit. Place the butter slices evenly on top. Bake for 35 to 40 minutes or until the cake is golden and the fruit is bubbling.

"My friend asked me if I wanted a frozen banana. I said 'No, but I want a regular banana later, so...yeah.'"

—Mitch Hedberg

Pineapple Carrot

The sunny taste of pineapple combines with rich carrot cake to make a fruity treat that is definitely out of the ordinary! The chopped nuts add crunch, and feel free to substitute pecans or almonds if you prefer.

2 (21-ounce) cans pineapple pie filling

1 box carrot cake mix

1/2 cup butter, sliced into 12 thin slices

1/2 cup chopped walnuts (optional)

Preheat the oven to 350 degrees F. Grease a 9 × 13-inch pan. Spread the pie filling on the bottom of the pan. Sprinkle the cake mix over the fruit. Evenly place the butter slices on top and sprinkle with the walnuts, if using. Bake for 35 to 40 minutes or until the cake is golden and the fruit is bubbling.

"Vegetables are a must on a diet. I suggest carrot cake, zucchini bread, and pumpkin pie."

—Jim Davis

Raspberry Red Velvet

A sweet red cake for your sweetheart, this is absolutely perfect for Valentine's Day, or any other time you want to show how much you care. Bursting with raspberry flavor and the delicious taste of red velvet cake, this four-ingredient showstopper will make you swoon!

2 (21-ounce) cans raspberry pie filling

1 (12-ounce) bag frozen raspberries, thawed

1 box red velvet cake mix

1/2 cup butter, sliced into 12 thin slices

Preheat the oven to 350 degrees F. Grease a 9 × 13-inch pan. Spread the pie filling on the bottom of the pan. Top with the raspberries. Sprinkle the cake mix over the fruit. Evenly place the butter slices on top. Bake for 35 to 40 minutes or until the cake is golden and the fruit is bubbling.

Apple Spice

A warm, spicy cake that is easier than apple cobbler but just as delicious! This quick-and-easy treat is a crowd-pleaser for potlucks and parties. There is something so comforting about apples, and this cake really lets them shine.

2 (21-ounce) cans apple pie filling

1 box spice cake mix

1/2 cup butter, sliced into 12 thin slices

Cinnamon sugar for topping

Preheat the oven to 350 degrees F. Grease a 9 × 13-inch pan. Spread the pie filling on the bottom of the pan. Sprinkle the cake mix over the fruit. Evenly place the butter slices on top. Sprinkle with cinnamon sugar. Bake for 35 to 40 minutes or until the cake is golden and the fruit is bubbling.

"If more of us valued food and cheer and song above hoarded gold, it would be a merrier world."

—J. R. R. Tolkien

Cherry Lemon-Lime

This recipe varies from my usual technique, swapping out the butter in favor of soda, which gives this cake a lemon-lime flavor and an extra dose of sweetness. Balance the sweetness by serving this cake with a tart lemon sorbet.

2 (21-ounce) cans cherry pie filling

1 box lemon cake mix

1 (12-ounce) can lemon-lime flavored soda

Preheat the oven to 350 degrees F. Grease a 9 × 13-inch pan. Spread the pie filling on the bottom of the pan. Sprinkle the cake mix over the fruit. Pour the soda evenly over the top. Bake for 35 to 40 minutes or until the cake is golden and the fruit is bubbling.

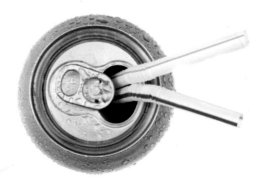

"Pie is the American synonym of prosperity, and its varying contents the calendar of the changing seasons."

—*New York Times*, 1902

Berry Orange

This summery treat is transformed into a year-round favorite through the convenience of frozen berries. The orange cake mix adds a citrus note that complements the berries, but feel free to substitute vanilla or lemon if you can't find orange cake mix.

1 (21-ounce) can strawberry pie filling

1 (15-ounce) bag frozen mixed berries, thawed

1 box orange cake mix

1/2 cup butter, sliced into 12 thin slices

Preheat the oven to 350 degrees F. Grease a 9 × 13-inch pan. Spread the pie filling on the bottom of the pan. Sprinkle the cake mix over the fruit. Evenly place the butter slices on top. Sprinkle with cinnamon sugar. Bake for 35 to 40 minutes or until the cake is golden and the fruit is bubbling.

"Summer afternoon—summer afternoon; to me those have always been the two most beautiful words in the English language."

—Henry James

Apricot Vanilla Almond

A sophisticated and beautiful dessert that you will be proud to show off for company, this cake combines delicious apricots with delicate vanilla and the crunch of slivered almonds. It is irresistible and elegant!

2 (21-ounce) cans apricot pie filling

1 box vanilla cake mix

1/2 cup butter, sliced into 12 thin slices

1/2 cup slivered almonds

Preheat the oven to 350 degrees F. Grease a 9 × 13-inch pan. Spread the pie filling on the bottom of the pan. Sprinkle the cake mix over the fruit. Evenly place the butter slices on top. Sprinkle the almonds over all. Bake for 35 to 40 minutes or until the cake is golden and the fruit is bubbling.

"Almond blossom, sent to teach us / That the spring days soon will reach us."
—Sir Edwin Arnold, "Almond Blossom"

Cranberry Spice

A delicious combination of two classic fall flavors—cranberries and spice cake. The cinnamon in the spice cake brings out the tart sweetness of the cranberries, making this a festive and attractive cake for any time of the year.

3 (14-ounce) cans whole-berry cranberry sauce

1 box spice cake mix

1/2 cup butter, sliced into 12 thin slices

Preheat the oven to 350 degrees F. Grease a 9 × 13-inch pan. Spread the cranberry sauce on the bottom of the pan. Sprinkle the cake mix over the fruit. Evenly place the butter slices on top. Bake for 35 to 40 minutes or until the cake is golden and the fruit is bubbling.

Pear Cranberry Vanilla

This cake offers the surprising but enormously satisfying combination of pears and cranberries, matched perfectly by rich vanilla cake. For all those times when you want something a little out of the ordinary, reach for this sweet and delicious dessert!

1 (15-ounce) can sliced pears in heavy syrup

1 (14-ounce) can whole-berry cranberry sauce

1 box vanilla cake mix

1/2 cup butter, sliced into 12 thin slices

Preheat the oven to 350 degrees F. Grease a 9 × 13-inch pan. Spread the pears and cranberry sauce on the bottom of the pan. Sprinkle the cake mix over the fruit. Evenly place the butter slices on top. Bake for 35 to 40 minutes or until the cake is golden and the fruit is bubbling.

Cranberry Apple

A classic combination that is perfect for Thanksgiving, or anytime when the cranberry craving hits! The ruby red color of this enticing cake just screams fall, and makes it a festive treat for any holiday gathering.

2 (21-ounce) cans apple pie filling

1 (14-ounce) can whole-berry cranberry sauce

1 box vanilla cake mix

1/2 cup butter, sliced into 12 thin slices

Preheat the oven to 350 degrees F. Grease a 9 × 13-inch pan. Spread the pie filling on the bottom of the pan, and spread the cranberry sauce on top. Sprinkle the cake mix over the fruit. Evenly place the butter slices on top. Bake for 35 to 40 minutes or until the cake is golden and the fruit is bubbling.

"Good food is very often, even most often, simple food."

—Anthony Bourdain

Blueberry Banana Nut

This fruity cake makes an excellent brunch treat, seeing as it combines three classic breakfast flavors. The nuts add a crunchy texture that contrasts well with the juicy berries and sweet cake.

2 (21-ounce) cans blueberry pie filling

1 box banana cake mix

1/2 cup butter, sliced into 12 thin slices

1/2 cup chopped walnuts or almonds

Preheat the oven to 350 degrees F. Grease a 9 × 13-inch pan. Spread the pie filling on the bottom of the pan. Sprinkle the cake mix over the fruit. Evenly place the butter slices on top and sprinkle with the nuts. Bake for 35 to 40 minutes or until the cake is golden and the fruit is bubbling.

Blueberry Lemon Almond

This cake is reminiscent of a classic blueberry coffee cake, but a whole lot easier to make! The blueberries highlight the lemon cake, and the crunch of almonds makes it a textural delight.

2 (21-ounce) cans blueberry pie filling

1 box lemon cake mix

1/2 cup butter, sliced into 12 thin slices

1/2 cup sliced almonds

Preheat the oven to 350 degrees F. Grease a 9 × 13-inch pan. Spread the pie filling on the bottom of the pan. Sprinkle the cake mix over the fruit. Evenly place the butter slices on top. Scatter the almonds over all. Bake for 35 to 40 minutes or until the cake is golden and the fruit is bubbling.

"When you die, if you get a choice between going to regular heaven or pie heaven, choose pie heaven. It might be a trick, but if it's not, mmmm, boy."
—Jack Handey

Pumpkin Pecan

The caramel cake mix and pecans give this cake a flavor that is like a cross between pumpkin pie and pecan pie—rich brown sugar, caramel, pumpkin, and toasty nuts create a decadent sweet treat.

1 (15-ounce) can pumpkin puree

1 (10-ounce) can evaporated milk

1 cup light brown sugar

3 large eggs

2 teaspoons pumpkin pie spice

1 box caramel cake mix

1 cup butter, melted

1/2 cup chopped pecans

Preheat the oven to 350 degrees F. Grease a 9 × 13-inch pan. Mix the pumpkin puree, evaporated milk, brown sugar, eggs, and pumpkin pie spice together in a bowl. Spread this mixture in the prepared pan. Sprinkle the cake mix evenly on top, and then drizzle the melted butter over everything. Scatter the pecans over all. Bake for 35 to 40 minutes or until the cake is golden and the fruit is bubbling.

"We must have a pie. Stress cannot exist in the presence of a pie."
—David Mamet, *Boston Marriage*

Blackberry Vanilla

You might have to search a little to find blackberry pie filling, but it is more than worth it to make this simple yet sensational cake. The juicy blackberries are set off perfectly by the vanilla cake. If you want to amp up the blackberry flavor, add some thawed frozen blackberries to the fruit before you add the cake mix.

2 (21-ounce) cans blackberry pie filling

1 box vanilla cake mix

1/2 cup butter, sliced into 12 thin slices

Preheat the oven to 350 degrees F. Grease a 9 × 13-inch pan. Spread the pie filling on the bottom of the pan. Sprinkle the cake mix on top of the fruit. Evenly place the butter slices on top. Bake for 35 to 40 minutes or until the cake is golden and the fruit is bubbling.

Peach Gingerbread

Peaches and ginger are one of the world's best flavor combinations, and this cake showcases it to high glory. With just three ingredients, you can create an impressive dessert that is perfect all year round.

2 (21-ounce) cans peach pie filling

1 box gingerbread cake mix

1/2 cup butter, sliced into 12 thin slices

Preheat the oven to 350 degrees F. Grease a 9 × 13-inch pan. Spread the pie filling on the bottom of the pan. Sprinkle the cake mix on top of the fruit. Evenly place the butter slices on top. Bake for 35 to 40 minutes or until the cake is golden and the fruit is bubbling.

"One cannot think well, love well, sleep well, if one has not dined well."
—Virginia Woolf

Cherry Corn Bread Pine Nut

This recipe has a unique twist: You swap cake mix for corn bread mix, creating a less sweet dessert with the satisfying crunch of cornmeal. The pine nuts add another delectable layer of texture to this elegant dessert.

2 (21-ounce) cans cherry pie filling

2 (8.5-ounce) boxes corn bread mix

1/2 cup butter, sliced into 12 thin slices

3 tablespoons pine nuts, toasted

Preheat the oven to 350 degrees F. Grease a 9 × 13-inch pan. Spread the pie filling on the bottom of the pan. Sprinkle the cake mix on top of the fruit. Evenly place the butter slices on top. Scatter the pine nuts over all. Bake for 35 to 40 minutes or until the cake is golden and the fruit is bubbling.

Sunshine

This cake is like the first sunny day after a long winter—bright and comforting! The pineapple and lemon combine to create a tangy and delicious treat that is amazing when topped with lemon sorbet.

2 (20-ounce) cans crushed pineapple

1 box lemon cake mix

1/2 cup butter, sliced into 12 thin slices

Preheat the oven to 350 degrees F. Grease a 9 × 13-inch pan. Spread the pie filling on the bottom of the pan. Sprinkle the cake mix over the fruit. Evenly place the butter slices on top. Bake for 35 to 40 minutes or until the cake is golden and the fruit is bubbling.

"In the depth of winter, I finally learned that within me there lay an invincible summer."

—Albert Camus

White Chocolate Raspberry

A pink-and-white masterpiece of rich white chocolate and ruby raspberries, this cake is the ultimate girls'-night-out dessert! Drape it in whipped cream and a drizzle of melted bittersweet chocolate for a truly over-the-top decadent dessert.

2 (21-ounce) cans raspberry pie filling

1 box white chocolate cake mix

1/2 cup butter, sliced into 12 thin slices

1 cup white chocolate chips

Preheat the oven to 350 degrees F. Grease a 9 × 13-inch pan. Spread the pie filling on the bottom of the pan. Sprinkle the cake mix over the fruit. Evenly place the butter slices on top. Sprinkle the white chocolate chips over all. Bake for 35 to 40 minutes or until the cake is golden and the fruit is bubbling.

CHAPTER TWO

CHOCOLATEY CAKES

Chocolate

The chocolate dump cakes have a slightly different technique than the fruit ones. Instead of pie filling, you make instant pudding and add the cake mix to it to create a fudgy, moist, unbelievably delicious chocolate dessert! It is very easy, but it tastes like it took all day. This basic version is the basis of the other chocolate recipes in the book, and is simple and scrumptious.

1 (5.9-ounce) box chocolate instant pudding mix

1 1/2 cups milk

1 box chocolate cake mix

1 1/2 cups chocolate chips

Preheat the oven to 350 degrees F. Grease a 9 × 13-inch pan. Prepare the chocolate pudding with the milk, according to the package directions. Mix in the dry cake mix and stir to combine. Spread the batter in the pan and sprinkle the chocolate chips on top. Bake for 30 minutes or until the cake is set and the edges pull away from the sides of the pan.

"Research tells us fourteen out of any ten individuals likes chocolate."
—Sandra Boynton

German Chocolate

Traditional German chocolate cake combines toasted coconut, pecans, and caramel in a luscious filling between chocolate cake layers. This easy dump cake version tops a chocolate cake with coconut, pecans, and a drizzle of caramel sauce—the coconut and pecans will toast in the oven as the cake bakes, so you skip a step!

1 (5.9-ounce) box chocolate instant pudding mix

1 1/2 cups milk

1 box chocolate cake mix

1 cup flaked coconut

1 cup chopped pecans

1 cup caramel sauce

Preheat the oven to 350 degrees F. Grease a 9 × 13-inch pan. Prepare the chocolate pudding with the milk according to the package directions. Mix in the dry cake mix and stir to combine. Spread the batter in the pan and sprinkle the coconut and pecans on top. Drizzle the caramel sauce over all. Bake for 30 minutes or until the cake is set and the edges pull away from the sides of the pan.

"My doctor told me to stop having intimate dinners for four unless there are three other people."

—Orson Welles

Salted Caramel Chocolate

A little sprinkle of sea salt takes caramel into the flavor stratosphere. If you love salted caramel, you will love this cake! It is a simple chocolate dump cake topped with caramel sauce and a light sprinkling of sea salt to add flavor and crunch.

1 (5.9-ounce) box chocolate instant pudding mix

1 1/2 cups milk

1 box chocolate cake mix

1 cup caramel sauce

1 teaspoon sea salt (like Maldon)

Preheat the oven to 350 degrees F. Grease a 9 × 13-inch pan. Prepare the chocolate pudding with the milk according to the package directions. Mix in the dry cake mix and stir to combine. Spread the batter in the pan and drizzle the caramel sauce on top. Sprinkle with the sea salt. Bake for 30 minutes or until the cake is set and the edges pull away from the sides of the pan.

"Salt is born of the purest of parents: the sun and the sea."   —Pythagoras

Chocolate Fudge Raspberry

A cake that gives an explosion of fresh raspberry flavor in every bite, gilded with deep chocolate! The best part about this cake is you can make it all year round, because with canned and frozen raspberries, it's always July.

2 (21-ounce) cans raspberry pie filling

1 (12-ounce) bag frozen raspberries, thawed

1 box chocolate cake mix

1/2 cup butter, sliced into 12 thin slices

1 1/2 cups chocolate chips

Preheat the oven to 350 degrees F. Grease a 9 × 13-inch pan. Spread the pie filling on the bottom of the pan. Scatter the raspberries on top. Sprinkle the cake mix on top of the fruit. Evenly place the butter slices on top. Scatter the chocolate chips over all. Bake for 35 to 40 minutes or until the cake is set and the fruit is bubbling.

"Seize the moment. Remember all those women on the *Titanic* who waved off the dessert cart."

—Erma Bombeck

Grasshopper Mint

If you have ever devoured a sleeve of Girl Scout Thin Mints, this is the cake for you. This easy cake tastes just like Thin Mints, but you don't have to wait for a Girl Scout to bring it to you! Delicious on its own, it is truly spectacular with a scoop of mint chocolate chip ice cream on top.

1 (5.9-ounce) box chocolate instant pudding mix

1 1/2 cups milk

1 box chocolate cake mix

1/2 teaspoon peppermint extract

1 1/2 cups chopped Andes candies or mint chocolate chips

Preheat the oven to 350 degrees F. Grease a 9 × 13-inch pan. Prepare the chocolate pudding with the milk, according to the package directions. Mix in the dry cake mix and peppermint extract and stir to combine. Spread the batter in the pan and sprinkle the Andes candies or mint chips on top. Bake for 30 minutes or until the cake is set and the edges pull away from the sides of the pan.

"After a good dinner one can forgive anybody, even one's own relatives."
—Oscar Wilde

Mocha Madness

What better flavor combination than coffee and chocolate? This sophisticated cake features both instant espresso powder (which you can buy at any grocery store these days) and a crunchy topping of chocolate-covered espresso beans. You can add them whole, chop them by hand, or even whir them in the food processor for a few seconds. Top with ice cream, hot fudge, and chopped nuts for an indulgent treat.

1 (5.9-ounce) box chocolate instant pudding mix

1 1/2 cups milk

1 teaspoon instant espresso powder

1 box chocolate cake mix

1 cup chocolate-covered espresso beans, chopped if desired

Preheat the oven to 350 degrees F. Grease a 9 × 13-inch pan. Prepare the chocolate pudding with the milk, according to the package directions. Mix in the espresso powder and dry cake mix and stir to combine. Spread the batter in the pan and sprinkle the chocolate-covered espresso beans on top. Bake for 30 minutes or until the cake is set and the edges pull away from the sides of the pan.

"There is no sincerer love than the love of food."   —George Bernard Shaw

Black Forest

Cherries and chocolate—what could be better? This delicious cake tastes like a chocolate covered cherry in a pan, and couldn't be easier to make. You'll note that the technique used here is the same for the fruit dump cakes, not the chocolate pudding ones in this chapter. Top this with whipped cream for a truly sensational treat!

2 (21-ounce) cans cherry pie filling

1 box chocolate cake mix

1/2 cup butter, sliced into 12 thin slices

1 cup chocolate chips

Preheat the oven to 350 degrees F. Grease a 9 × 13-inch pan. Spread the pie filling on the bottom of the pan, and sprinkle the cake mix on top. Evenly place the butter slices on top and sprinkle the chocolate chips over all. Bake for 35 to 40 minutes or until the fruit is bubbling and the cake is set.

"People who love to eat are always the best people."   —Julia Child

Caramel Turtle

This cake pays homage to old-time candy shop caramel turtles. With crunchy nuts and chewy caramel all drenched in chocolate, it's a showstopper. Store-bought caramel sauce makes this a cinch to throw together at the last minute, and you can use any kind of nuts you like.

1 (5.9-ounce) box chocolate instant pudding mix

1 1/2 cups milk

1 box chocolate cake mix

1 1/2 cups roasted, salted cashews, almonds, or macadamia nuts

1 cup caramel sauce

Preheat the oven to 350 degrees F. Grease a 9 × 13-inch pan. Prepare the chocolate pudding with the milk, according to the package directions. Mix in the dry cake mix and stir to combine. Spread the batter in the pan and sprinkle the nuts on top. Drizzle the caramel sauce over all. Bake for 30 minutes or until the cake is set and the edges pull away from the sides of the pan.

S'Mores

This easy cake takes the flavor of a classic s'more and puts it in a dump cake, starting with a layer of graham crackers at the bottom! If you like, you can add some chopped milk chocolate to the top to give it even more of a s'mores-like flavor. No campfire required!

6 whole graham crackers

1 (5.9-ounce) box chocolate instant pudding mix

1 1/2 cups milk

1 box chocolate cake mix

1 1/2 cups miniature marshmallows

Preheat the oven to 350 degrees F. Grease a 9 × 13-inch pan. Lay the graham crackers on the bottom of the pan, breaking them if necessary to fit. Prepare the chocolate pudding with the milk, according to the package directions. Mix in the dry cake mix and stir to combine. Spread the batter over the graham crackers and sprinkle the marshmallows on top. Bake for 30 minutes or until the cake is set and the edges pull away from the sides of the pan.

"First you take the graham, you stick the chocolate on the graham. Then you roast the 'mallow. When the 'mallow's flaming, you stick it on the chocolate. Then cover with the other end. Then you scarf." *The Sandlot*

Black-and-White

There is nothing better than the black-and-white cookies you find in New York City, and every time I visit, I buy a dozen to bring home. This easy cake will recreate the delicious look and flavor of those classic cookies. The white chocolate chips and marshmallows give this cake an arresting contrast and sweet vanilla complement to the dark chocolate cake.

1 (5.9-ounce) box instant chocolate pudding mix

1 1/2 cups milk

1 box chocolate cake mix

1 cup white chocolate chips

1 cup miniature marshmallows

Preheat the oven to 350 degrees F. Grease a 9 × 13-inch pan. Prepare the chocolate pudding with the milk, according to the package directions. Mix in the dry cake mix and stir to combine. Spread the batter in the pan and sprinkle the white chocolate chips and marshmallows on top. Bake for 30 minutes or until the cake is set and the edges pull away from the sides of the pan.

"A balanced diet is a cookie in each hand."   —Barbara Johnson

Chocolate Coconut Almond

If you like Almond Joy candy bars, you will love this cake. If you wish, you can add a little almond extract to the cake batter for a more pronounced almond flavor, or mix it up by using salted almonds for an appealing salty-sweet combination.

1 (5.9-ounce) box instant chocolate pudding mix

1 1/2 cups milk

1 box chocolate cake mix

1 cup whole roasted unsalted almonds

1 cup flaked coconut

1 cup milk chocolate chips

Preheat the oven to 350 degrees F. Grease a 9 × 13-inch pan. Prepare the chocolate pudding with the milk, according to the package directions. Mix in the dry cake mix and stir to combine. Spread the batter in the pan and sprinkle the nuts, coconut, and chocolate chips on top. Bake for 30 minutes or until the cake is set and the edges pull away from the sides of the pan.

Milk Chocolate Bar

Some people swear by dark chocolate, but there is a special place for the sweet, creamy flavor of milk chocolate. Like a classic Hershey's Kiss, this cake celebrates milk chocolate in all its glory, and is divine served with chocolate whipped cream.

1 (5.9-ounce) box instant chocolate pudding mix

1 1/2 cups milk

1 box milk chocolate cake mix

4 (6.2 ounces) milk chocolate bars, chopped

Preheat the oven to 350 degrees F. Grease a 9 × 13-inch pan. Prepare the chocolate pudding with the milk, according to the package directions. Mix in the dry cake mix and stir to combine. Spread the batter in the pan and sprinkle the chocolate on top. Bake for 30 minutes or until the cake is set and the edges pull away from the sides of the pan.

"Do you think because you are virtuous, that there shall be no more cakes and ale?"

– Twelfth Night

M&M

Okay, this one is pretty simple, but just in case it hasn't occurred to you to blanket a cake with M&M's, now you have no excuse! The crunchy candy and extra boost of chocolate flavor made this a favorite among my recipe testers, despite how easy it is to whip up. You can use peanut, pretzel, or other flavor M&M's if you prefer—crunchy pretzel is always a crowd-pleaser!

1 (5.9-ounce) box instant chocolate pudding mix

1 1/2 cups milk

1 box chocolate cake mix

1 1/2 cups M&M's

Preheat the oven to 350 degrees F. Grease a 9 × 13-inch pan. Prepare the chocolate pudding with the milk, according to the package directions. Mix in the dry cake mix and stir to combine. Spread the batter in the pan and sprinkle the M&M's on top. Bake for 30 minutes or until the cake is set and the edges pull away from the sides of the pan.

Chocolate Peanut Butter Chip

There is something about the slightly sandy texture and true peanut butter flavor of this cake that is addictive. It couldn't be simpler to make, and you can add some salted cocktail peanuts or chocolate-covered peanuts along with the chips if you want a stronger peanut flavor.

1 (5.9-ounce) box instant chocolate pudding mix

1 1/2 cups milk

1 box chocolate cake mix

1 1/2 cups peanut butter chips

Preheat the oven to 350 degrees F. Grease a 9 × 13-inch pan. Prepare the chocolate pudding with the milk, according to the package directions. Mix in the dry cake mix and stir to combine. Spread the batter in the pan and sprinkle the peanut butter chips on top. Bake for 30 minutes or until the cake is set and the edges pull away from the sides of the pan.

Peanut Butter Explosion

This cake is like a peanut butter cup on steroids! The addition of a layer of chunky peanut butter hidden inside the cake makes for a happy, delicious surprise, and the added crunch of salted cocktail peanuts really puts this over the edge. The best part is that it is so simple to make that you can whip it up anytime your craving for chocolate and peanut butter hits!

1 (5.9-ounce) box instant chocolate pudding mix

1 1/2 cups milk

1 box chocolate cake mix

2 cups chunky peanut butter

1 1/2 cups salted cocktail peanuts

Preheat the oven to 350 degrees F. Grease a 9 × 13-inch pan. Prepare the chocolate pudding with the milk, according to the package directions. Mix in the dry cake mix and stir to combine. Spread half of the batter in the pan. Spread the peanut butter on top of the batter. Top with the remaining cake batter and spread evenly. Sprinkle with the peanuts. Bake for 30 minutes or until the cake is set and the edges pull away from the sides of the pan.

"We all eat, and it would be a sad waste of opportunity to eat badly."
—Anna Thomas

Chocolate Cherry Cola

Chocolate and cherry cola are a classic and delicious flavor combination! This three-ingredient marvel is fruity, sweet, and chocolaty, with a soda-fountain appeal that will delight kids and adults. To amp up the cherry flavor, feel free to use cherry cola instead of regular.

2 (21-ounce) cans cherry pie filling

1 box chocolate cake mix

1 (12-ounce) can cola

Preheat the oven to 350 degrees F. Grease a 9 × 13-inch pan. Spread the pie filling on the bottom of the pan, and sprinkle the cake mix on top. Pour the cola evenly over all. Bake for 35 to 40 minutes or until the fruit is bubbling and the cake is set.

Chocolate-Covered Strawberry

This winner is a perfect Valentine's Day treat, especially if you serve it with a chocolate-dipped strawberry on top! You can also add frozen sliced strawberries to the fruit layer to make an even juicier, fruity cake with more fresh strawberry flavor.

2 (21-ounce) cans strawberry pie filling

1 box chocolate cake mix

1/2 cup butter, sliced into 12 thin slices

1 cup chocolate chips

Preheat the oven to 350 degrees F. Grease a 9 × 13-inch pan. Spread the pie filling on the bottom of the pan, and sprinkle the cake mix on top. Evenly place the butter slices on top and sprinkle the chocolate chips over all. Bake for 35 to 40 minutes or until the fruit is bubbling and the cake is set.

CHAPTER THREE

SAUCES AND TOPPINGS

5-Minute Hot Fudge Sauce

You would never know from tasting this thick, rich sauce that it comes together in 5 minutes! Why buy the stuff in the jar when you can have homemade sauce that tastes a hundred times better in 5 minutes? I love quick-and-easy recipes (obviously), but this sauce is well worth the minimal effort And you can make it in the microwave, so there is no pan to wash.

3/4 cup heavy cream

1/3 cup light corn syrup

1/2 cup brown sugar

1/3 cup cocoa powder

1/2 teaspoon salt

6 ounces bittersweet chocolate chips

1/4 cup butter, cut into small pieces

1 teaspoon vanilla extract

In a microwave-safe bowl or large glass measuring cup, stir together the cream, corn syrup, brown sugar, cocoa powder, and salt. Microwave on high for 1 to 1 1/2 minutes, or until the mixture is hot but not boiling. Add the chocolate chips and butter and stir until melted and smooth. Add the vanilla and mix well. Store any leftovers in a tightly closed container in the refrigerator, and reheat in 10-second bursts in the microwave until it is pourable.

YIELD: ABOUT 2 CUPS

"Always serve too much hot fudge sauce on hot fudge sundaes. It makes people overjoyed and puts them in your debt."

—Judith Olney

Easy Caramel Sauce

Several recipes in this book call for caramel sauce, and you can certainly use the bottled stuff. But this caramel sauce tastes a lot better, and is easy to make, so once in a while you might want to pull out all the stops and do it yourself.

1 cup packed dark brown sugar

1/2 cup half-and-half

1/4 cup butter

1/8 teaspoon salt

1 tablespoon vanilla extract

Heat the brown sugar, half-and-half, butter, and salt in a heavy saucepan over medium-low heat. Stir constantly until the sugar is dissolved and the sauce thickens, about 5 minutes. Stir in the vanilla and cook for 1 minute more. Remove the pan from the heat and cool the sauce slightly. Store any leftovers in a tightly closed container in the refrigerator, and reheat in 10-second bursts in the microwave until the sauce is pourable.

YIELD: ABOUT 1 1/2 CUPS

Marshmallow Sauce

A topping so easy to make that you won't believe how good it tastes poured over chocolate ice cream or dump cake! Just two ingredients and a couple of minutes at the stove, and you have a homemade sauce that will dress up many of the cakes in this book. Really, what cake wouldn't benefit from a hit of sticky vanilla sweetness?

1 1/2 cups Marshmallow Fluff

3 tablespoons water

Heat the Marshmallow Fluff and water in a small saucepan over medium-low heat until melted and combined. Remove the pan from the heat and cool slightly. Store leftovers in a tightly closed container in the refrigerator and microwave in 10-second bursts to achieve your desired consistency.

YIELD: ABOUT 1 CUP

Boozy Butterscotch Sauce

This thick, sticky sauce is slightly different from the Easy Caramel Sauce, as it doesn't contain any butter, includes corn syrup for chewiness, and has the added boost of booze from Scotch whiskey. Any blended whiskey will do—you don't need to use your expensive single-malt here. You will find this sauce is a miracle on cakes like Pumpkin Pecan or Apple Spice, as well as a serious treat poured over vanilla ice cream.

1 1/2 cups dark brown sugar

1/2 cup light corn syrup

1/4 cup water

1 teaspoon salt

3/4 cup heavy cream

2 tablespoons Scotch whiskey

1/2 teaspoon vanilla extract

Heat the brown sugar, corn syrup, water, salt, and heavy cream in a heavy saucepan over medium-low heat until the sugar dissolves and the sauce is thickened, about 5 minutes. Add the whiskey and vanilla and simmer for another 2 minutes. Remove the pan from the heat and cool slightly. Store any leftovers in a tightly sealed container in the refrigerator and reheat any left-over sauce in 10-second bursts in the microwave until you reach the desired consistency.

YIELD: ABOUT 2 1/2 CUPS

"Invention, my dear friends, is 93% perspiration, 6% electricity, 4% evaporation, and 2% butterscotch ripple."

—Willy Wonka

Homemade Whipped Cream

There is something special about whipping cream from scratch—it tastes amazing, and it's surprisingly fast and simple for something so decadent. It is also a lot thicker and more stable than the aerated stuff in a can, so you can even use it to frost a cake. Be sure to use the largest bowl you have (metal is best, because it is cold, which will help the cream take shape faster) to minimize splattering.

1 cup cold heavy cream

2 tablespoons sugar
(adjust to the sweetness level you prefer)

1 teaspoon vanilla extract

In a large mixing bowl, whip the cream and sugar with a whisk or electric hand mixer until thick and the cream holds stiff peaks when you raise the whisk or beater. Add the vanilla and whisk briefly to incorporate. Serve immediately.

YIELD: ABOUT 2 CUPS

"Ice cream is exquisite. What a pity it isn't illegal."   —Voltaire

Chocolate Whipped Cream

This fluffy cloud is created by folding cooled melted chocolate into whipped cream, which further stiffens it, making it an ideal frosting for any kind of cake, as well as a delicious topping for ice cream or dump cakes!

1 cup cold heavy cream

2 tablespoons sugar

1 teaspoon vanilla extract

1/2 cup semisweet chocolate chips, melted and cooled

In a large mixing bowl, whip the cream and sugar with a whisk or electric hand mixer until thick and the cream holds stiff peaks when you raise the whisk or beater. Add the vanilla and whisk briefly to incorporate. With a rubber spatula, fold in the cooled melted chocolate until well incorporated, being careful not to deflate the whipped cream. Serve immediately.

YIELD: ABOUT 2 1/2 CUPS

Coffee Whipped Cream

This topping is perfect for the Mocha Madness cake, and you can even add it to some of the fruit cakes, especially Apple Cinnamon. It is a simple way to add extra flavor to whipped cream. Use regular instant coffee if you don't have any espresso powder.

1 cup cold heavy cream

1 teaspoon instant espresso powder

2 tablespoons sugar

In a large mixing bowl, stir the heavy cream and espresso powder together until the espresso powder dissolves. Add the sugar and whip the mixture with a whisk or electric hand mixer until it's thick and holds stiff peaks when you raise the whisk or beater. Serve immediately.

YIELD: ABOUT 2 CUPS

"I'd rather take coffee than compliments just now."
—Louisa May Alcott, *Little Women*

Raspberry Sauce

An elegant, ruby-red sauce that can create an inviting pool for many of the cakes in this book! The best thing about this sauce is that it can give a splash of fresh raspberry flavor any time of year, since it uses frozen berries. Keeping a frozen bag of raspberries on hand is great if you want to make a last-minute dessert—just thaw them in the microwave and in a few minutes, you can have a sweet, homemade sauce to drizzle on cake or ice cream.

1 (12-ounce) bag frozen unsweetened raspberries, thawed

1/4 cup sugar, or to taste

Place the raspberries in a fine-meshed strainer over a large bowl and press on them with the back of a spoon, forcing the juice and flesh into the bowl, until all that remains in the strainer is the seeds. Stir in the sugar until dissolved, taste, and add more sugar, if desired. Store in a tightly closed container in the refrigerator.

YIELD: ABOUT 3/4 CUP

"Without ice cream, there would be darkness and chaos."   —Don Kardong

Peanut Butter Sauce

A luscious, creamy sauce that is as easy as stirring a pan for a few minutes! The peanut butter lovers in your house will go crazy for this thick, sweet sauce, which is the perfect topping for a plain chocolate cake as well as Chocolate Peanut Butter Chip or Peanut Butter Explosion. Any leftovers can be reheated and poured over ice cream for an instant homemade treat.

1 cup creamy peanut butter

3/4 cup heavy cream

1/3 cup sugar

1/4 cup light corn syrup

Put all the ingredients in a small, heavy saucepan and stir over medium-low heat until melted and combined. Continue cooking for a few more minutes until the sugar is dissolved and the sauce is smooth. Remove the pan from the heat and cool slightly. Store any leftovers in a tightly closed container in the refrigerator and reheat in 10-second bursts in the microwave until your desired consistency is reached.

YIELD: ABOUT 1 3/4 CUPS

BONUS!

MUG CAKE RECIPES FROM

BEST MUG CAKES EVER

AVAILABLE EVERYWHERE BOOKS ARE SOLD!

BEST
MUG
CAKES
EVER

TREAT YOURSELF TO

HOMEMADE CAKE FOR ONE

IN FIVE MINUTES OR LESS

monica sweeney

Chocolate-Covered Pretzel

The salty-sweet combination of chocolate-covered pretzels meets the comfort of cake. The contrasting crunch they give to the soft cake makes for a texturally interesting treat that will have you craving more!

4 tablespoons self-rising flour

4 tablespoons sugar

3 tablespoons cocoa powder

2 tablespoons beaten egg or liquid egg substitute

3 tablespoons milk

2 tablespoons vegetable oil

1/2 teaspoon vanilla extract

5 small chocolate-covered pretzels, broken into pieces

Mix the flour, sugar, and cocoa powder in a mug. Add the egg, milk, oil, and vanilla and stir until well combined. Fold in the chocolate-covered pretzels. Microwave on high for 1 minute or until the top is just dry.

"To eat is a necessity, but to eat intelligently is an art."
—François de La Rochefoucauld

Lime Coconut

A tropical breeze in a mug, this cake is full of sweet coconut and zesty lime flavor. It's great served with some sliced mango or fresh pineapple, and makes a refreshing, not-too-sweet treat perfect for summertime.

4 tablespoons self-rising flour

3 tablespoons sugar

1/4 teaspoon lime zest

2 tablespoons shredded sweetened coconut

2 tablespoons beaten egg or liquid egg substitute

3 tablespoons milk

2 tablespoons vegetable oil

Mix the flour, sugar, lime zest, and coconut in a mug. Add the egg, milk, and oil and stir until well combined. Microwave on high for 1 minute or until the top is just dry.

"I love food that carries food. Run, waiter, before I eat you too."
—Jarod Kintz, *Love Quotes for the Ages. Specifically Ages 19–91.*

INDEX